ATKINS DIET COOKBOOK

THE COMPLETE BEGINNER'S GUIDE WITH 4 WEEKS MEAL PLAN TO LOSE WEIGHT AND FEEL GREAT

THERESA GORDON

CONTENTS

COPYRIGHT

INTRODUCTION

The Atkins diet is one of the most popular diets out there, and it's no surprise. It's a diet where you can eat lots of bacon and cheese and still lose weight. Low-carbohydrate diets like the Atkins Diet are a good way to lose weight because your body can break down fat cells much easier than it can break down the fat in carbohydrate cells. Low-carb diets also make your body more responsive to insulin, which means that your body will use the insulin it produces more effectively.

The main principle of the Atkins diet is an almost complete rejection of carbohydrates and, in particular, from sugar (in any form). Thus, the production of insulin is reduced, which, as you know, plays a major role in the formation and accumulation of fats in the body. At the same time, the breakdown and assimilation of protein foods require a lot of energy - which, in the absence of carbohydrates, the body simply has nowhere else to take, as soon as from the already accumulated fat reserves.

Perhaps sometime after the start of the Atkins diet, you'll get fed up with the protein menu - it's completely natural, the body will start to desperately ask for carbohydrates, which means that thoughts about cabbage salad, vegetable stew, apples, and berries, etc. will sound more and more in your head .P. It is important to resist during this carbohydrate "starvation" - further, each stage of the Atkins diet will be much easier than the last one. In general terms, the Atkins diet scheme is as follows: the whole diet is divided into four stages. The first stage takes about two weeks; the duration of the second and third stages is calculated individually, depending on the dynamics of weight loss. The task of the second and third stages of the Atkins diet is to understand how many carbohydrates will be critical for weight loss. For this, it is necessary to strictly and thoroughly fix the number of carbohydrates in which weight stabilization begins, and in which – it's first, even insignificant, increase. The last, final stage is needed to consolidate the results.

BREAKFAST

BASIL STUFFED CHICKEN BREASTS

Preparation time: 20 minutes

Cooking Time: 45 minutes

Serving: 4

Ingredients:

- 2 - bone-in, skin-on chicken breasts, 2 - tbsp. cream cheese
- 2 - tbsp. shredded cheese, ¼ - tsp. garlic paste
- 3-4 - fresh basil leaves finely chopped, black pepper

Directions:

1. Preheat the oven to 375F.
2. Make the stuffing by joining the cream cheddar, cheddar, garlic paste, basil, and dull pepper.
3. Carefully strip back the skin on one side of the chicken chest and detect the half stuffing inside.
4. Smooth it down and supersede the skin
5. Repeat for the other piece of chicken.

6. Cook on a getting ready plate for 45 minutes or until the inward temperature of 165F has been come to.

Nutrition:

- Calories 152g,
- Fat 15g
- Carbs 8g
- Sugar 12g
- Protein 22g

LOW CARB PORK MEDALLIONS

Preparation time: 15 minutes

Cooking Time: 30 minutes

Serving: 4

Ingredients:

- 1 - lb. pork tenderloin
- 3 - medium shallots (chopped nice), ¼ - cup oil

Directions:

1. Diminish the hamburger into half-inch thick cuts.
2. Hack the shallots and notice them on a plate.
3. Warm the oil in a skillet press every piece of red meat into the shallots on the two angles.
4. Detect the hamburger cuts with shallots into the warm oil and get ready supper till achieved.
5. You will find that a piece of the shallots will expand for the

span of cooking. At the same time, they'll even now present delightful taste to the meat.

6. Essentially cook supper the red meat until it's cooked through.
7. Present with veggies.

Nutrition:

- Calories 53g
- Fat 5g, Carbs 1g
- Sugar 2g
- Protein 6g

EASY MOZZARELLA & PESTO CHICKEN CASSEROLE

Preparation time: 30 minutes

Cooking Time: 30 minutes

Serving: 4

Ingredients:

- ¼ - cup pesto, 8 - oz. cream cheese softened
- ¼ - ½ - cup heavy cream
- 8 - oz. mozzarella cubed
- 2 - lb. cooked cubed chicken breasts
- 8 - oz. mozzarella shredded

Directions:

1. Preheat stove to 400. Sprinkle a tremendous supper dish with a cooking shower.
2. Unite the underlying three fixings and mix them until smooth in a bread bowl.

3. Incorporate the chicken and cubed mozzarella. Trade to the goulash dish.
4. Sprinkle the decimated mozzarella to complete the process of everything.
5. Plan for 25-30 minutes. Present with zoodles, spinach, or squashed cauliflower

Nutrition:

- Calories 452g
- Fat 26g,
- Carbs 11g
- Sugars 5g,
- Protein 39g

STUFFED CHICKEN WITH ASPARAGUS & BACON

Preparation time: 5 minutes

Cooking Time: 40 minutes

Serving: 8

Ingredients:

- 8 - Chicken tenders about 1 lb.
- ½ - tsp. salt , ¼ - tsp. pepper
- 12 - Asparagus spears about .5 lb.
- 8 - Pieces bacon about .5 lb.

Directions:

1. Preheat oven to 400.
2. Spot 2 chook tenders to complete the system of the whole lot.
3. Season with pretty salt and pepper.
4. Incorporate three spears of asparagus.
5. Overlay the bacon over the fowl and asparagus to shield every piece of it together.

6. Warmth for 40mins until the hen is cooked through, the asparagus is clean, and the bacon is new.

Nutrition

- Calories 152g,
- Fat 15g
- Carbs 8g
- Sugar 12g
- Protein 22g

LUNCH

KETO HAMBURGER

Preparation Time: 15 minutes

Cooking Time: 70 minutes

Servings: 4

Ingredients:

- For the burger buns:
- Two cups almond flour
- Five tbsps. ground psyllium husk powder
- Two tsp. baking powder
- One tsp. salt
- 1&1/2 cup water
- Two tsp. cider vinegar
- Three egg whites
- One tbsp. sesame seed
- For the hamburger:
- Two pounds beef
- 1-ounce olive oil
- Pepper and salt

- 1&1/2-ounce lettuce
- One tomato
- One red onion
- Half cup mayonnaise
- Five ounces bacon

Directions:

1. Warm-up your oven at 150 degrees.
2. Mix the listed dry items for the buns in a bowl. Boil the water. Put egg whites, water, and vinegar to the dry mix. Mix.
3. Make individual pieces of buns, put sesame seeds on the top. Bake for sixty minutes
4. Fry the slices of bacon. Keep aside.
5. Mix beef, pepper, and salt in a bowl. Make patties. Grill the beef patties for five minutes, each side.
6. Combine mayonnaise and lettuce in a bowl. Cut the buns in half. Add beef patty, lettuce mix, onion slice, and a tomato slice. Top with bacon slices. Serve.

Nutrition:

- Calories: 1070.3
- Protein: 53.4g
- Carbs: 6.1g
- Fat: 85.3g
- Fiber: 12.3g

CHICKEN WINGS AND BLUE CHEESE DRESSING

Preparation Time: 70 minutes

Cooking Time: 25 minutes

Servings: 4

Ingredients:

- One-third cup mayonnaise
- One-fourth cup sour cream
- Three tsp. lemon juice
- One-fourth tsp. of each:
- Salt
- Garlic powder
- Half cup whipping cream
- Three ounces blue cheese
- For the chicken wings:
- Two pounds chicken wings
- Two tbsps. olive oil
- One-fourth tsp. garlic powder
- One clove garlic

- One-third tsp. black pepper
- One tsp. salt
- Two ounces parmesan cheese

Directions:

1. Mix all the blue cheese dressing items in a bowl. Chill within forty minutes.
2. Combine the chicken with olive oil and spices. Marinate for thirty minutes.
3. Bake in the oven for twenty-five minutes. Toss the chicken wings with parmesan cheese in a bowl.
4. Serve with blue cheese dressing by the side.

Nutrition:

- Calories: 839.3
- Protein: 51.2g
- Carbs: 2.9g
- Fat: 67.8g
- Fiber: 0.2g

SALMON BURGERS WITH LEMON BUTTER AND MASH

Preparation Time: 70 minutes

Cooking Time: 15 minutes

Servings: 4

Ingredients:

- For the salmon burgers:
- Two pounds salmon
- One egg
- Half yellow onion
- One tsp. salt
- Half tsp. black pepper
- Two ounces butter
- For the green mash:
- One-pound broccoli
- Five ounces of butter
- Two ounces parmesan cheese
- Pepper
- salt

- For the lemon butter:
- Four ounces butter
- Two tbsps. lemon juice
- Pepper
- salt

Directions:

1. Warm-up your oven at 100 degrees.
2. Cut the salmon into small pieces. Combine all the burger items with the fish in a blender. Pulse for thirty seconds. Make eight patties.
3. Warm-up butter in an iron skillet. Fry the burgers for five minutes.
4. Boil water, along with some salt in a pot, put the broccoli florets. Cook for three to four minutes. Drain. Add parmesan cheese and butter. Blend the ingredients using an immersion blender. Add pepper and salt.
5. Combine lemon juice with butter, pepper, and salt. Beat using an electric beater.
6. Put a dollop of lemon butter on the top and green mash by the side. Serve.

Nutrition:

- Calories: 1025.3
- Protein: 44.5g
- Carbs: 6.8g
- Fat: 90.1g
- Fiber: 3.1g

BARBECUED RIBS

Preparation Time: 15 minutes

Cooking Time: 1 hour & 10 minutes

Servings: 4

Ingredients:

- One-fourth cup Dijon mustard
- Two tbsps. of each:
- Cider vinegar
- Butter
- Salt
- Three pounds of spare ribs
- Four tbsps. paprika powder
- Half tbsp. chili powder
- 1&1/2 tbsp. garlic powder
- Two tsp. of each:
- Onion powder
- Cumin
- Two & 1/2 tbsp. black pepper

Directions:

1. Warm-up a grill for thirty minutes.
2. Mix vinegar and Dijon mustard in a bowl, put the ribs and coat.
3. Mix all the listed spices. Rub the mix all over the ribs. Put aside. Put ribs on an aluminum foil. Add some butter over the ribs. Wrap with foil. Grill within one hour. Remove and slice.
4. Put the reserved spice mix. Grill again within ten minutes. Serve.

Nutrition:

- Calories: 980.3
- Protein: 54.3g
- Carbs: 5.8g
- Fat: 80.2g
- Fiber: 4.6g

TURKEY BURGERS AND TOMATO BUTTER

Preparation Time: 15 minutes

Cooking Time: 15 minutes

Servings: 4

Ingredients:

- For the chicken patties:
- Two pounds of chicken
- One egg
- Half onion
- One tsp. salt
- Half tsp. black pepper
- One a half tsp. thyme
- Two ounces butter
- For the fried cabbage:
- Two pounds green cabbage
- Three ounces butter
- One tsp. salt
- Half tsp. black pepper (ground)

- For the tomato butter:
- Four ounces butter
- One tbsp. tomato paste
- One tsp. red wine vinegar
- Pepper
- salt

Directions:

1. Warm-up your oven at 100 degrees.
2. Combine the listed items for the patties in a large bowl. Shape the mixture into patties.
3. Fry the chicken patties for five minutes, each side. Keep warm in the oven.
4. Warm-up butter in a pan. Put the cabbage, plus pepper and salt. Fry for five minutes.
5. Whip the items for the tomato butter in a bowl using an electric mixer.
6. Serve with a dollop of tomato butter from the top.

Nutrition:

- Calories: 830.4
- Protein: 33.6g
- Carbs: 6.7g
- Fat: 71.5g
- Fiber: 5.1g

DINNER

BRUSSELS SPROUTS WITH BACON

Preparation Time: 15 minutes

Cooking Time: 40 minutes

Servings: 6

Ingredients:

- Bacon (16 oz.)
- Brussels sprouts (16 oz.)
- Black pepper

Directions:

1. Warm the oven to reach 400° Fahrenheit.
2. Slice the bacon into small lengthwise pieces. Put the sprouts and bacon with pepper.
3. Bake within 35 to 40 minutes. Serve.

Nutrition:

- Carbohydrates: 3.9 grams
- Protein: 7.9 grams
- Total Fats: 6.9 grams
- Calories: 113

BUN LESS BURGER - KETO STYLE

Preparation Time: 15 minutes

Cooking Time: 25 minutes

Servings: 6

Ingredients:

- Ground beef 1 lb.
- Worcestershire sauce 1 tbsp.
- Steak Seasoning 1 tbsp.
- Olive oil 2 tbsp.
- Onions 4 oz.

Directions:

1. Mix the beef, olive oil, Worcestershire sauce, and seasonings.
2. Grill the burger. Prepare the onions by adding one tablespoon of oil in a skillet to med-low heat. Sauté. Serve.

Nutrition:

- Carbohydrates: 2 grams
- Protein: 26 grams
- Total Fats: 40 grams
- Calories: 479

COFFEE BBQ PORK BELLY

Preparation Time: 15 minutes

Cooking Time: 60 minutes

Servings: 4

Ingredients:

- Beef stock 1.5 cups
- Pork belly 2 lb.
- Olive oil 4 tbsp)
- Low-carb barbecue dry rub
- Instant Espresso Powder 2 tbsp.

Directions:

1. Set the oven at 350° Fahrenheit.
2. Heat-up the beef stock in a small saucepan.
3. Mix in the dry barbecue rub and espresso powder.
4. Put the pork belly, skin side up in a shallow dish and drizzle half of the oil over the top.

5. Put the hot stock around the pork belly. Bake within 45 minutes.
6. Sear each slice within three minutes per side. Serve.

Nutrition:

- Net Carbohydrates: 2.6 grams
- Protein: 24 grams
- Total Fats: 68 grams
- Calories: 644

GARLIC & THYME LAMB CHOPS

Preparation Time: 15 minutes

Cooking Time: 10 minutes

Servings: 6

Ingredients:

- Lamb chops 6 - 4 oz.
- Whole garlic cloves 4
- Thyme sprigs 2
- Ground thyme 1 tsp.
- Olive oil 3 tbsp.

Directions:

1. Warm-up a skillet. Put the olive oil. Rub the chops with the spices.
2. Put the chops in the skillet with the garlic and sprigs of thyme.
3. Sauté within 3 to 4 minutes and serve.

Nutrition:

- Net Carbohydrates: 1 gram
- Protein: 14 grams
- Total Fats: 21 grams
- Calories: 252

JAMAICAN JERK PORK ROAST

Preparation Time: 15 minutes

Cooking Time: 4 hours

Servings: 12

Ingredients:

- Olive oil 1 tbsp.
- Pork shoulder 4 lb.
- Beef Broth .5 cup
- Jamaican Jerk spice blend .25 cup

Directions:

1. Rub the roast well the oil and the jerk spice blend. Sear the roast on all sides. Put the beef broth.
2. Simmer within four hours on low. Shred and serve.

Nutrition:

- Net Carbohydrates: 0 grams
- Protein: 23 grams
- Total Fats: 20 grams
- Calories: 282

DESSERT

CINNAMON SOUR CREAM COFFEE CAKE

Preparation time: 10 minutes

Cooking Time: 45 minutes

Serving: 12

Ingredients:

- 2 cups of almond flour
- 1tablespoons of baking powder
- ¼ teaspoon of baking soda
- cups of sugar substitute
- Two eggs
- 2teaspoons of cinnamon
- ¼ teaspoon of salt
- ¼ teaspoon of nutmeg
- One stick of butter (1/2 cup)
- 1 cup of sour cream
- For the topping:
- 1 cup of almond flour
- One stick of butter

- ½ cup of coconut flour
- Two teaspoons of cinnamon
- ½ cup of sugar substitute
- ½ cup of pecans
- ¼ teaspoon of salt

Directions

1. Preheat your oven to 350° F.
2. Grease a 10-inch, spring-form cake pan with butter.
3. Begin by making the topping. In a bowl, mix the sugar substitute, coconut flour, almond flour, ground cinnamon, pecans, and salt.
4. Slice one butter stick into thin pieces. Add the details to the dry mixture. Mix to form crumbs and set aside.
5. In another bowl, mix the almond flour, baking powder, sugar substitute, spices, and salt.
6. Thaw a stick of butter and let it cool.
7. Now combine the melted butter with the eggs and sour cream, blending well.
8. Mixture the butter mixture into the dry mixture to create your cake batter. Mix well and spread in the cake pan.
9. Sprinkle the crumb topping over the batter.
10. Bake the cake for forty-five minutes to one hour. Allow the cake to cool and serve.

Nutrition:

- Calories 283
- Fat 28.5 g
- Protein 5.9 g
- Carbohydrates 7.1 g
- Fiber 3.1. G
- Sugar 1.9 g

CINNAMON CHOCOLATE SMOOTHIE

Preparation time: 10 minutes

Cooking Time: 35 minutes

Serving: 1

Ingredients:

- ¾ cup of coconut milk
- Two teaspoons of cacao powder, unsweetened
- ½ ripe avocado
- One teaspoon of cinnamon powder
- sweetener to taste
- ¼ teaspoon of vanilla extract
- ½ teaspoon of coconut oil (optional)

Directions

1. Blend all of the ingredients in your blender or food processor and enjoy it.

Nutrition

- Calories 300
- Fat 30 g
- Protein 3 g
- Carbohydrates 14 g
- Sugar 2 g
- Fiber 10 g

CREAM SODA (PHASE 1)

Preparation time: 10 minutes

Cooking Time: 5 minutes

Serving: 1

Ingredients:

- 1 cup diet vanilla soda
- 1 tbsp. heavy cream
- 2 tbsp. whipped cream cheese

Directions

1. Combine whipped cream cheese and heavy cream in a small bowl. Whip until combined and fluffy.
2. Spoon cream cheese and massive cream mixture into the bottom of a glass. Fill the rest of the glass with vanilla soda.

Nutrition:

THERESA GORDON

- 150Cal.,
- 36gCarbs

BLACKBERRY YOGURT NUTS
(PHASE 2)

Preparation time: 10 minutes

Cooking Time: 1hr minutes

Serving: 2

Ingredients:

- 1 cup plain, unsweetened Greek yogurt
- 10 Macadamia nuts
- 1/2 cup fresh blackberries

Directions

1. In a food processor, combine yogurt and nuts until paste forms.
2. Combine pasta and blackberries in a small bowl, mixing them gently until combined.
3. Lay coated blackberries out on a baking sheet in a single layer and refrigerate for 1 hour.

Nutrition:

- Calories 43
- Total Carbohydrate 10 g
- Dietary fiber 5 g
- Sugar 4.9 g
- Protein 1.4 g

CHERRY PLUM BREAD PUDDING (PHASE 3)

Preparation time: 15 minutes

Cooking Time: 45 minutes

Serving: 2

Ingredients:

- 1 TBS. butter
- 6 slices whole-wheat bread, stale
- Three ripe plums, chopped
- 1 cup pitted cherries
- 2 cups unflavored almond milk
- Four eggs, beaten
- 1 tsp. cinnamon
- 4 TBS. cream cheese

Directions

1. Preheat oven to 350 degrees. Grease the bottom and sides of a

9"x13" pan with butter. Arrange torn chunks of bread over the bottom of the pan.
2. In a large mixing bowl, combine fruit, milk, eggs, cinnamon, and cream cheese. Whip together until well combined.
3. Pour mixture over bread, and bake for 45 minutes, or until the top is well browned.

Nutrition:

- 341 calories;
- total fat 11g;
- saturated fat 5g;

2 WEEKS MEAL PLAN

Days

Breakfast

Lunch

Dinner

Dessert

1

Breakfast Burrito

Turkey Burgers and Tomato Butter

Brussels Sprouts With Bacon

Cinnamon Sour Cream Coffee Cake

2

Stuffed Chicken With Asparagus & Bacon

Keto Hamburger

Bun less Burger - Keto Style

Cinnamon Chocolate Smoothie

3

Basil Stuffed Chicken Breasts

Chicken Wings and Blue Cheese Dressing

Coffee BBQ Pork Belly

Cream Soda (Phase 1)

4

Low Carb Pork Medallions

Salmon Burgers with Lemon Butter and Mash

Garlic & Thyme Lamb Chops

Blackberry Yogurt Nuts (Phase 2)

5

Easy Mozzarella & Pesto Chicken Casserole

Barbecued Ribs

Jamaican Jerk Pork Roast

Cherry Plum Bread Pudding (Phase 3

6

Breakfast Burrito

Turkey Burgers and Tomato Butter

Brussels Sprouts With Bacon

Cinnamon Sour Cream Coffee Cake

7

Stuffed Chicken With Asparagus & Bacon

Keto Hamburger

Bun less Burger - Keto Style

Cinnamon Chocolate Smoothie

8

Basil Stuffed Chicken Breasts

Chicken Wings and Blue Cheese Dressing

Coffee BBQ Pork Belly

Cream Soda (Phase 1)

9

Low Carb Pork Medallions

Salmon Burgers with Lemon Butter and Mash

Garlic & Thyme Lamb Chops

Blackberry Yogurt Nuts (Phase 2)

10

Easy Mozzarella & Pesto Chicken Casserole

Barbecued Ribs

Jamaican Jerk Pork Roast

Cherry Plum Bread Pudding (Phase 3

11

Breakfast Burrito

Turkey Burgers and Tomato Butter

Brussels Sprouts With Bacon

Cinnamon Sour Cream Coffee Cake

12

Stuffed Chicken With Asparagus & Bacon

Keto Hamburger

Bun less Burger - Keto Style

Cinnamon Chocolate Smoothie

13

Basil Stuffed Chicken Breasts

Chicken Wings and Blue Cheese Dressing

Coffee BBQ Pork Belly

Cream Soda (Phase 1)

14

Low Carb Pork Medallions

Salmon Burgers with Lemon Butter and Mash

Garlic & Thyme Lamb Chops

Blackberry Yogurt Nuts (Phase 2)

AFTERWORD

Thanks for reading to the end. Some people find it fairly easy to cut back on carbs and have great success without any problems on the Atkins diet. Other people, however, have more difficulty switching to the Atkins diet. It can be a surprise to go from eating much of your caloric intake in carbs to moving to a very low-carb diet, but with the following keys to success, you will be able to transition more smoothly.

First, make sure to make the best use of your net carbs. Remember, net carbs are the total number of carbohydrates in your food minus the dietary fiber. The remainder is the net carb for that food. Since fiber has almost no impact on your blood sugar, it is not necessary to cut down fiber. It is best to get your complete allotment of net carbs, especially in phase 1. Make sure you eat all your net carbs.

Second, make sure to eat plenty of vegetables. In phase 1, most of your net carbs (12 to 15 grams) will be found in the vegetables that you eat. The next step will talk more about what vegetables you should consume in each phase of the diet.

Make sure to keep salt in your diet. As your body transitions from carb-burning for energy to fat burning, if you do not get enough salt, you may suffer from headaches, lightheadedness, cramps, or a feeling of weakness or lethargy. By making sure that there is adequate sodium intake, you should be able to avert these symptoms as your body adapts to the new way of eating.